BATHROOMS & BEDROOMS

BETA-PLUS

BATHROOMS & BEDROOMS

February 2008
ISBN 13: 978 90 77213 88 9

CONTENTS

FOREWORD

Following the success of the titles "BATHROOMS" and "BEDROOMS", published in this home-design series over three years ago, we have decided to create an entirely new edition for 2008, which combines these two themes in one book.

After all, bathrooms and bedrooms form a whole, and so should be designed in complementary styles. Increasingly, these rooms are united in one single space, with the emphasis on well-being, calm and serenity, in a luxurious en-suite atmosphere.

All of the bathroom and bedroom projects featured here have been photographed recently, especially for this book.
The reader will also find information about the design of these rooms, which are essential in every home, including both classic, timeless styles and more streamlined, contemporary interiors.

The projects featured in these many illustrated reports exemplify recent trends and provide inspiring examples for the design of modern bedrooms and bathrooms.

Wim Pauwels
Publisher

p. 12-13
A project by
Esther Gutmer.

An 'aksent project.

PART I

TIMELESS BATHROOMS AND BEDROOMS

A COMBINATION OF TRADITIONS

The Themenos architects tend to feel a certain responsibility for the lifestyle of the people who live in their buildings.

Bathrooms and bedrooms are often the most important rooms in the house: they should combine to form a refuge, as people spend such a great deal of time sleeping and bathing.

The modern bathroom is a combination of conflicting traditions: from the purely functional sanitary space of days gone by to contemporary design and comfort.

It is essential for everything in a bathroom to be stored within easy reach. The lighting must be in keeping with the function of the room and, together with the colour palette, provide helpful direction for users of the space.

Increasingly, the bathroom is also becoming a place for relaxation and its design must reflect this new role.

The modern bedroom is a calm counterpart to the busy study: a private space where we can be ourselves, in an atmosphere of comfort and well-being, both physical and spiritual.

Harmonious proportions created by vertical stripes of equal widths and different colours. The stripes bring balance into this space and add a formal accent to the casual atmosphere.

Wallpaper is in fashion again: it creates a feeling of cosiness in a room.

The wood panelling here offers a feeling of intimacy and comfort. The sanded finish lends a fresh note to this space.

Wood panelling has also been installed in the children's room, ensuring a sense of warmth and safety.

THEMENOS cvba

Sint-Jansvliet 8
B – 2000 Antwerp
T +32 (0)3 248 49 93
F +32 (0)3 248 56 23
www.themenos.be

A MASTER OF SPACES

Created in 1996 by interior designer Gilles de Meulemeester, the Ebony shop and design practice have become unrivalled benchmarks in interior design.

From renovation to pure concepts, Gilles de Meulemeester has carried out numerous conversions on private houses in Belgium, Paris, the south of France, London, Geneva, Berlin, Moscow, even in Aspen, Colorado.
We also owe him recognition for the redesign of restaurant Les Etangs Mellaerts, Havana Corner, the creation of the trendy Rouge Tomate as well as the classic restaurant Vieux Boitsfort.

In parallel with the interior design side, Ebony also offers the public a wide range of original furniture collections, decorative articles and objects.
Famous names, selected for their quality and their compatibility with the house philosophy, can be found in the shop on Avenue Louise (Promemoria, Modenature, Ecart International, Armani Casa,...) in settings which bear the unmistakable imprint of the personality of this master of spaces.

And because Gilles de Meulemeester is particularly attached to the notion of "Belgian quality", Ebony also carries an exclusive range of furniture designed in collaboration with Belgian craftsmen (Amalgam, Interni Edition, Carré d'As) which can be custom modified.

EBONY bvba
Gilles de Meulemeester
    132 av. Louise
    B – 1050 Brussels
    T +32 (0)2 646 86 02
    F +32 (0)2 649 52 61

    64 Boulevard Malesherbes
    F – 75008 Paris
    T +33 (0)1 42 93 75 06

    www.ebony-interiors.com
    ebony@ebony-interiors.com

A CLASSICAL,
LUXURIOUS FEELING

The owners of this Boston property were looking for a classical, luxurious feeling.

Architect Bruce Bananto realized this in collaboration with EA2, a company specialized in working with high end european architectural antiques.

Natural materials as wood, Italian Carrara marble, and Belgian Blue Heaven are used to create a timeless look.

Old Carrara marble in combination with glass and chrome fittings are the main materials in this luxurious shower.

The master bedroom in a restful color palette. Architect Bruce Bananto choose for an oak floor from the Cosy Collection by Old Historical Plank. The Old Historical Plank collection, the antique fireplace and furniture used, are distributed by HuntForAntiques.com

BRUCE BANANTO
    145 W. 28th ST.
    Suite 803
    New York, NY 10001
    T +1 212 563 1750
    F +1 646 416 6218

EA2
European Architectural Antiques
    26 Heistgoorstraat
    B – 2220 Antwerpen / Heist op den Berg
    T +1 617 894 04 95
    info@ea2.be

HUNTFORANTIQUES.COM
    4 Itegembaan
    B – 2580 Antwerp / Putte
    T +32 (0)477 56 03 38

A SENSUAL TOUCH

With a style that is both contemporary and authentic, architect Hans Verstuyft integrated this newly built house into its historic surroundings: a country setting near the River Scheldt.

The bathroom was designed as a harmonious space, with the stone finish providing a sensual touch, such as one might find in a spa.

The freestanding bath is by the window, lending an extra dimension to relaxing in the tub. The heating is concealed within the wall units. The shelves have both a decorative and a practical purpose, and create a more relaxed look in the bathroom.

HANS VERSTUYFT ARCHITECTS

Van Bréestraat 35
B-2018 Antwerp
T +32 (0)3 485 6762
F +32 (0)3 485 6764
www.hansverstuyftarchitecten.be
mail@hansverstuyftarchitecten.be

The natural-stone finish has been extended to the washbasins and shower, giving the bathroom a look that is soft and robust. Alongside the rain shower head is a light channel with indirect lighting.

AN OASIS OF WELL-BEING
IN A RENOVATED CASTLE

The studio of Vittorio Simoni created the entire interior-design concept for this renovated castle in Belgian Limburg.

Simoni transformed the vaulted cellar to create an oasis of calm and well-being.

The bedrooms and bathrooms in this unique project radiate a sense of serenity and classic contemporary elegance.

The work in natural stone was carried out by Van den Weghe.
Jozef Reynaerts provided the soft furnishings and decorative touches.

The vaulted cellar of this renovated castle has been converted into a fitness and relaxation space.
This photo shows the entrance to the sauna and shower.
The small window ensures daylight from the garden: half of the basement is above ground level.

The toilet, shower, corridors and washstand are all finished in the same natural stone by Van den Weghe.
The bush-hammered finish was chosen not only for its anti-slip properties, but also for aesthetic reasons: the roughness of the floor forms a fine contrast with the brick and marlstone vaulting.
The shower is in the same stone throughout, with polished edges. Only the central section, where people have to walk, has a bush-hammered anti-slip finish.

p. 44-45
A view of the relaxation corner. Cushions in Pierre Frey fabrics (by Jozef Reynaerts).
The entrance to the shower and sauna is set at an angle.
This gives it a greater volume that is in proportion with the architecture of the vaulted cellar.
Stairs and floor are all by Van den Weghe with a bush-hammered finish.

p. 46-47
A view of the two built-in Jacuzzis.
One Jacuzzi is built to accommodate six seated people, whilst the other has space for two people to lie.
Both Jacuzzis are in Bisazza mosaic.
The technical equipment for drainage and heating is built into the surround.
The rear wall is in sandstone coloured to harmonise with the marlstone.
The built-in Kreon spotlights create the right atmosphere.

Each suite consists of a bathroom, dressing room and bedroom. This bathroom presents an interplay of light and architectural forms. The materials used in this space are quarter-cut oak with a dark stain (Williams & Koch), in combination with Lea Tecnoquartz ceramic tiles in silver. The vanity unit has a lacquered finish.

The entrance hall and bathroom corridor is in oak parquet with a dark stain.

The wall units are also in oak veneer, stained in the same colour as the floor.

The lower level, the sleeping area, has a border of dark-stained parquet around

a central section in carpet by Van Besouw.

p. 52-53
Blue is the only touch of
colour in this room. It is
subtly reflected in the
soft furnishings and the
blue leather of the
Promemoria stool.
Fabrics by Jozef
Reynaerts.

A bathroom with an Antonio Lupi washstand.

The large mirrored cabinet gives a more spacious feel to this narrow bathroom.

The units are in oak veneer, with a dark stain matching the colour of the wooden floor in the bedroom.

A large shower with two walls and floor in Lea Tecnoquartz silver ceramic tiles, and a glass screen that provides the necessary transparency. The stainless-steel handle incorporated into this screen reinforces and protects the glass and can also be used as a towel rail.

Kreon lighting.

Two bedrooms and their bathrooms.

The floors are in dark-stained oak parquet. The furniture is also in oak veneer, stained in the same colour as the parquet (Williams & Koch).

A Duravit vessel washbasin was selected for the bathroom.

Paintwork in stucco; a combination of indirect lighting and built-in spots creates a beautiful atmosphere.

The existing radiators were retained.

p. 58-59

The master bedroom.
The freestanding dresser provides storage space and creates a partition between the sleeping area and the circulation zone. Promemoria lamps.
The opposite wall houses the television; the two alcoves serve as frames for paintings. The recessed sections on the left and right are finished in gold leaf.
Wooden parquet in dark-tinted wood runs around the room, surrounding a pale carpet from the Van Besouw collection.
Bespoke handles by Vervloet to match the colours and materials of the Lithos switches and Promemoria table lamps.

The master bathroom is situated in the tower of the castle: the alcove above the door was part of the original tower.

Both the surrounds of the door and the alcove above it are finished in gold leaf.

Floor in French stone, units in stained oak veneer, washbasins in the same natural stone as the floor. The large shower has side jets, a hand-held attachment and a large rain-shower head by Dornbracht. The existing radiators were retained in this room as well.

SIMONI

Hentjenslaan 9-11

B – 3511 Hasselt

T +32 (0)11 25 35 02

F +32 (0)11 87 21 00

www.simoni.be

simoni@simoni.be

VAN DEN WEGHE

The Stone Company

Statiestraat 69

B – 9870 Zulte

T +32 (0)9 388 83 00

F +32 (0)9 388 51 66

www.vandenweghe.be

info@vandenweghe.be

TIMELESS ELEGANCE

Costermans Villa Projects coordinates construction and interiors for top-quality country houses and residences, particularly in the leafy outskirts of Antwerp.

Bathrooms and bedrooms are always a most important aspect of their interiors.

This report features the bathrooms in one house and the bathrooms and bedrooms in another home. The theme running through these projects is the timeless sense of elegance that both radiate: one of the many selling points of this high-class construction company from Schilde.

The bath and sinks are in tongue-and-groove MDF. Floor and surfaces in Portuguese Branco de Mos stone. Plastic stools by Quinze & Milan.

The master bathroom with made-to-measure floor and surface in Branco de Mos; units in French oak veneer and lacquered MDF. Chrome-plated taps by Dornbracht.

Double shower in Branco de Mos slabs and chrome-plated RVB taps.

Floors in Branco de Mos; shower wall in marble mosaic.

A child's bedroom in playful shades of blue and brown, combined with an oak desk and bedside tables.

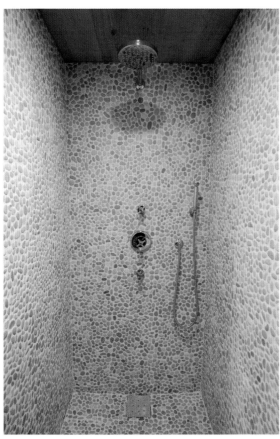

The shower is in beige pebbles. RVB taps.

p. 72-73
The dominant shade in the guestroom is a warm red. Lamps by Stéphane Davidts.

p. 74-75
The master bedroom with an oak table at the foot of the bed and sturdy oak feet under the bed. Lighting by Stéphane Davidts and Terzani.

The guest bathroom
with a combination of
Crema Marfil marble and
a shower in tumbled
marble mosaic.
A splash-resistant
flatscreen TV. Tradition
taps by Damixa.

The sauna is in abachi wood. Washing unit by Duravit with taps by RVB.

COSTERMANS VILLA PROJECTS
Dwarsdreef 52
B – 2970 Schilde
T +32 (0)3 385 02 44
F +32 (0)3 384 29 66
www.costermans-projecten.be
info@costermans-projecten.be

SOBER AND SERENE

In this report, interior architect Alexis Herbosch (Apluz design studio) presents a renovation project in Wilrijk.

The main bedroom/bathroom/dressing-room area of this house was designed in a muted harmony of white and écru, combined with a touch of dark brown in the bedroom.

By demolishing a wall, Alexis Herbosch created a connection between two separate rooms.
Pivoting doors close off the rooms and create different atmospheres.

The washbasins have been placed on streamlined blocks. The taps are in an unconventional position on the front of the units. The central block serves as a storage shelf.

The shower is clad
with pebbles.

Both of the doors in the wall behind the bath can be opened to create an
atmosphere of space.

With the doors closed, these rooms appear to be completely separate.

The bath (Wall Strip by Aquamass) is the eye-catching feature in this design: its
lines (almost the shape of a curling leaf) merge seamlessly with the white wall
behind.

The floor is in pine planks with a pale finish.

White wardrobes in the dressing room with open shelves in the centre.

A white-painted walk-in dressing room in this chocolate-brown room, creating a strong contrast.

Apluz (creative group)
Alexis Herbosch
Interior architect
        Van Noortstraat 31
        B-2018 Antwerp
        T +32(0)3 293 60 04
        F +32(0)3 293 60 05
        www.apluz.be
        contact@apluz.be

A bath with a view of the roof terrace. The wooden blinds are in dark stained wood.

p. 86-87
The master bedroom is a white room with accents in dark stained oak. The existing fireplace was retained.
Bed in chocolate brown.

ENGLISH INSPIRATION

Costermans Villa Projects created the master bedroom with en-suite bathroom and dressing room and the guest bathroom in this exclusive country house in the leafy outskirts of Antwerp.

The atmosphere in these rooms matches the look throughout the rest of the house: classic elegance that is undeniably English in inspiration.

The floor of this English-style bathroom is in aged Rosso Verona, surrounded by made-to-measure Bianco Perlino.

A vanity unit for two, and also a two-person shower in beige marble mosaic.

Belgian taps, 1935 series by RVB in nickel.

p. 92-93

The spacious bedroom

combines classic

English-style furniture

and a fresh atmosphere.

The floor and shower walls in this guest
bathroom are tiled in marble mosaic.
Dressing room with hand-painted panel doors,
a leather surface and a vanity table in the same
French oak as the floor.

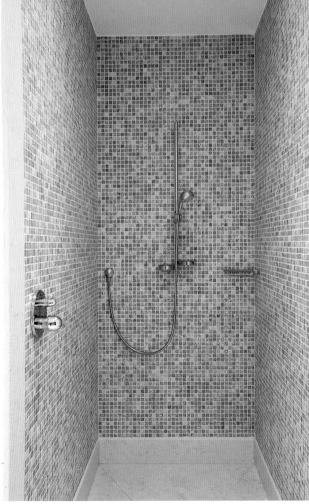

COSTERMANS VILLA PROJECTS
Dwarsdreef 52
B – 2970 Schilde
T +32 (0)3 385 02 44
F +32 (0)3 384 29 66
www.costermans-projecten.be
info@costermans-projecten.be

CALMNESS AND CLASS

De Menagerie is renowned mainly for its exclusive kitchen designs, but this company from Aalst also designs complete interiors, in which bathrooms are an important element.

This report features one of De Menagerie's recent bathroom projects: a harmonious combination of wood and natural stone, suffused by an atmosphere of calmness and class.

De Menagerie always works with top-quality materials and
exclusive accessories, such as taps by Volevatch.
Natural stone works: Van den Weghe.

DE MENAGERIE
Luc Lormans

Leo de Bethunelaan 45
B – 9300 Aalst
T +32 (0)53 78 69 39
F +32 (0)53 70 79 96
MOB +32 (0)475 76 84 15
www.demenagerie.be
info@demenagerie.be

TIMELESS CLASS

Van den Weghe (The Stone Company) supplied all of the stonework for this project by Themenos.

This is a very special project involving exclusive Greek marble (Yellow Leaf and Golden Brown) and tumbled mosaic pieces.

The wooden panelling creates a feeling of warmth and cosiness.

Van den Weghe fitted the main bathroom in
Greek Yellow Leaf marble.
The clefts in the floor of the walk-in shower
allow the water to drain away.

The shower is in tumbled mosaic tiles: the technique of tumbling gently wears down the corners and edges, giving them the same finish as the surface.

VAN DEN WEGHE

The Stone Company

    Statiestraat 69

    B – 9870 Zulte

    T +32 (0)9 388 83 00

    F +32 (0)9 388 51 66

    www.vandenweghe.be

    info@vandenweghe.be

THEMENOS cvba

    Sint-Jansvliet 8

    B – 2000 Antwerp

    T +32 (0)3 248 49 93

    F +32 (0)3 248 56 23

    www.themenos.be

The children's bathroom is finished in Golden Brown marble.

ELEGANCE AND CRAFTMANSHIP

In 1996, Anne De Visscher and her husband Eric Meert started designing and creating traditionally built kitchens, bathrooms and complete interiors in a timeless style.

All of these projects conform to the highest standards of quality: every piece of furniture is made to order and adapted to the wishes of the client.

During the installation, the furniture is hand-painted to harmonise with the colour palette of the house.

In this report, Il Etait Une Fois present a number of recently completed bathrooms and bedrooms.

IL ETAIT UNE FOIS ...

Place du Châtelain, 10
B – 1050 Brussels
T +32 (0)2 537 07 05
F +32 (0)2 537 63 07
MOB +32 (0)475 787 133 (Anne De Visscher)
+32 (0)475 488 713 (Eric Meert)
+32 (0)476 50 44 21 (Catherine Mahieu)
www.iletaitunefois.be
iletaitunefois@skynet.be

Van Bunnenlaan 10
B – 8300 Knokke

AN ATMOSPHERE OF WARMTH

For this interior project, Obumex worked together with the stone company Van den Weghe.

The company's exclusive stone combines with wood to ensure an atmosphere of warmth.

The Ghibli anciento granite is first treated with a Bunsen burner and roughened, after which steel brushes are used to give the surface a velvet-smooth finish that also has excellent anti-slip properties.

VAN DEN WEGHE

The Stone Company
  Statiestraat 69
  B – 9870 Zulte
  T +32 (0)9 388 83 00
  F +32 (0)9 388 51 66
  www.vandenweghe.be
  info@vandenweghe.be

OBUMEX

  www.obumex.be
  design@obumex.be

EXCLUSIVE TAPS AND BATHROOM ACCESSORIES

Waterl'Eau is the original name for an unusual bathroom shop that has been based on Schuttershofstraat in Antwerp since 1993.
The company recently opened a second shop on Naamsestraat in Brussels.

Ineke Tap and her team present exclusive taps, washbasins and all kinds of bathroom accessories that are hard to find elsewhere.

One of Waterl'Eau's success stories is the distribution of Volevatch products.

This French producer of top-quality taps and bathroom accessories has in recent decades become the benchmark for interior architects and other designers of beautiful luxury bathrooms, both in contemporary and more classic, timeless styles.

This report, in which Waterl'Eau introduce a contemporary and a more classic bathroom project with Volevatch taps, clearly illustrates the many possibilities of Volevatch products.

p. 118-123

The bathroom on p. 118 and p. 120-123 is a design by interior architect Marianne Swyzen.

She selected Volevatch taps from the Bistrot range, which harmonise perfectly with the white Carrara marble and the wooden floor.

p. 124-126

Volevatch Bistrot taps were also chosen for this project, but in a completely different context: the owner of this country home is passionate about antiques and old construction materials, so chose Volevatch for its timeless appeal.

Visitors to the branches of
Waterl'Eau will find a wealth
of exclusive taps and
bathroom accessories,
a. o. from Czech & Speake.

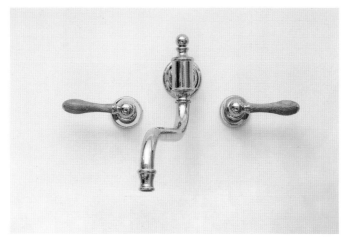

WATERL'EAU

    Schuttershofstraat 47 (1st floor, by appointment)

    B – 2000 Antwerp

    T +32 (0)3 226 75 86

    F +32 (0)3 226 75 93

    info@waterleau-shop.be

    Naamsestraat 9

    B – 1000 Brussels

    T/F +32 (0)2 513 24 00

    waterleau-bxl@skynet.be

    www.waterleau-shop.be

THE BATHROOMS AND BEDROOMS OF NANTUCKET LODGE

This distinctive house, built in solid wood by Mi Casa, has already received a detailed profile in our new title "Living with Wood" (February 2008).

This report focuses on the bathrooms and bedrooms of this very special house.

As in the other rooms in the house, the work involved close collaboration with Lerou Ijzerwaren for the finishing touches: authentic door knobs and handles, hinges and locks, switches and bathroom fixtures.

The owner of this house drew inspiration from three holiday atmospheres: De Haan (a seaside resort in Belgium) for the bathroom; Nantucket (USA) for the bedroom, whirlpool bath and sauna; and the French island of Ile de Ré for the guest toilet and bathroom.

Lerou was founded in 1792, making it one of the oldest firms in Belgium. The company specialises in trimmings for doors and furniture, authentic, restored fittings and exclusive interior accessories, produced by traditional methods and with a passion for authenticity.

A porthole window from Lerou in the centre of the photograph.

The door furniture, hinges and locks, switch plates, and other accessories, are all available from Lerou.

Lighting and mirror from Lerou's Nantucket collection.
Accessories from the China Blue collection and solid fittings with a chrome finish. Thermostatic shower with a hand-held attachment and a 300mm rain-shower head. Luxury four-hole bath tap from the Fairfield collection.

A porcelain washbasin in Belle-Époque style with high-tech taps and solid accessories.

All of the products can be made by Lerou in any of the company's finishes, including door fittings, switch plates, grilles for new ventilation systems, and many other accessories.

An authentic porcelain handle and back plate with "vase anglaise" split hinges. A Nautique wall lamp and toilet accessories in nickel; handmade washbasin and an authentic tap with ceramic interior.

LEROU

Monnikenwerve 131
Industriezone Blauwe Toren
B – 8000 Brugge
T +32 (0)50 31 74 42
F +32 (0)50 31 01 60
www.lerou.com
info@lerou.com

PART II

CONTEMPORARY INSPIRATION

TIMELESS AND CONTEMPORARY

The bathrooms and bedrooms in this house in Waasmunster, created by Martine Cammaert (C&C Designburo), are designed in a style that is both timeless and contemporary.

The combination of durable wood and natural stone has resulted in a sophisticated interior that radiates an atmosphere of calm and serenity.

A combination of standard floor tiles with made-to-measure slabs on the walls and a Pietra Piasentina washbasin surround. A design by C&C Designburo, with stonework carried out by Van den Weghe.

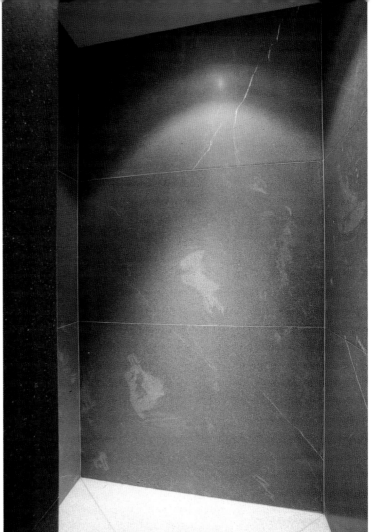

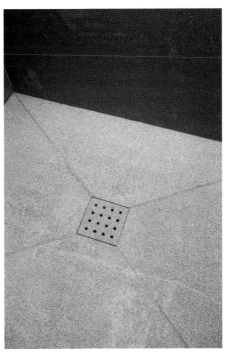

Wardrobes in painted MDF. The horizontal lines reinforce the sense of space
and the connection between the bathroom and the dressing room.

C&C DESIGNBURO
Martine Cammaert
　　　Alfons Minoodtlaan 8
　　　B – 9030 Mariakerke
　　　T +32 (0)9 227 03 79
　　　F +32 (0)9 227 78 29
　　　c.c.designburo@skynet.be

A HARMONY OF
BLACK AND WHITE

Cy Peys Interior Architects followed a principle of neutrality when creating this loft-type bathroom in the Zuidkwartier district of Antwerp.
Sturdy, distinctive materials were used throughout.

The black mosaic and smoked glass are in contrast with the industrial character of the building.

The parquet floor of the adjoining bedrooms extends into this bathroom, creating a sense of continuity.

Bath and toilet by Duravit; Hansgrohe taps.

CY PEYS

Interior architects

Timmerwerfstraat 1

B – 2000 Antwerp

T +32 (0)3 248 67 50

F +32 (0)3 248 39 55

www.cypeys.com

info@cypeys.com

SLEEK AND STREAMLINED, WARM AND COSY

In this project by Dennis T'Jampens (the renovation of a house in Knokke), one theme ran through the entire interior concept and was extended into the bathroom: sleek and streamlined, but also warm and cosy.

The aim was to turn a small bathroom into a large bathing space with a completely different atmosphere and an appropriate colour scheme.
This new bathroom was designed to be a place where the client could rest and relax.
The combination of Massangis natural stone, beige tadelakt, bronze/brown glass and a few chrome touches has created an atmosphere that is streamlined and yet cosy and calming, completely in line with the renovation of the rest of the house.

Beneath the roof window was the ideal spot for this Starck-designed bath: it offers a fine view and beautiful natural light, further accentuated by the shutters.
Perfect drainage and installation of pipes and electricity was made possible by the use of a special floor section that also serves to separate the parquet floor (which runs through from the bedroom) and the French Massangis sandstone, which seamlessly flows into the washbasin surround, forming a harmonious unit.
Mem taps by Dornbracht in a chrome finish.

The lighting is also a very important element of the final look. Dennis
T'Jampens selected floor lighting to create a calm, almost mysterious effect.

DTJ-INTERIOR ARCHITECT
Dennis T'Jampens
Opstal 37
B - 2650 Edegem
MOB +32 (0) 479 805 179
www.dtj-interiorarchitect.be
dennis@dtj-interiorarchitect.be

AN OASIS OF CALM

Interior architect Filip Vanryckeghem (iXtra) created an oasis of calm in the upstairs corridor, bathrooms and bedrooms of this distinctive house.

D&D Interieur from Deerlijk (Kurt Dejaeger) were responsible for the overall interior of the house.

Van den Weghe (The Stone Company) selected and installed the stonework.

Wood and natural stone flow together seamlessly, creating a warm and cosy atmosphere.

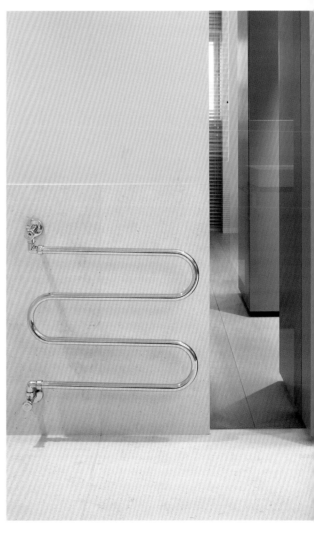

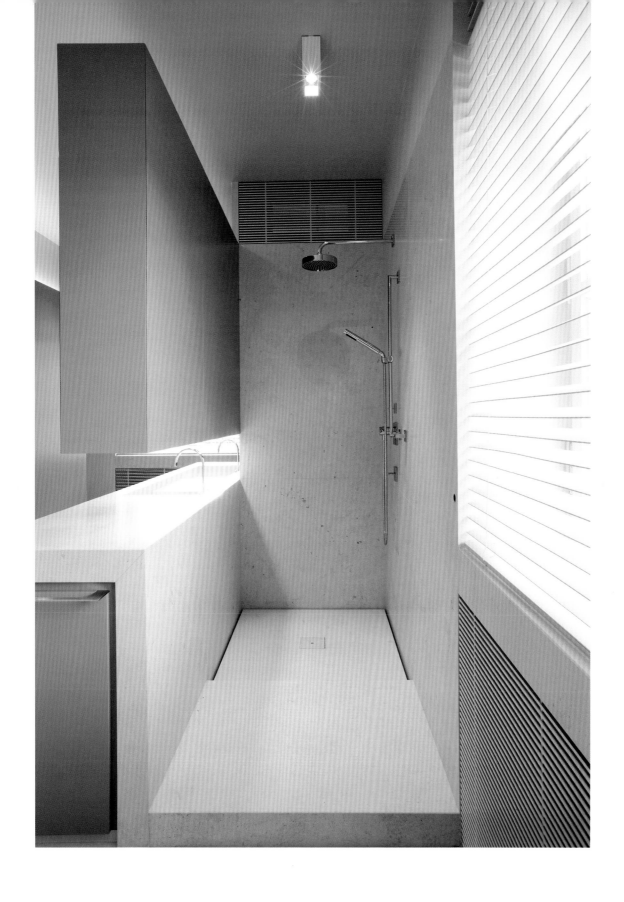

IXTRA Interior Architecture

Filip Vanryckeghem

    Ieperstraat 18

    B – 8930 Menen

    T/F +32 (0)56 530 457

    www.ixtra.be

    info@ixtra.be

VAN DEN WEGHE

The Stone Company

    Statiestraat 69

    B – 9870 Zulte

    T +32 (0)9 388 83 00

    F +32 (0)9 388 51 66

    www.vandenweghe.be

    info@vandenweghe.be

A HARMONY OF WOOD AND BIANCO STATUARIO MARBLE

Interior architect Filip Vanryckeghem (iXtra) designed the plan for this attic room with an en-suite bathroom and shower.

He came up with a surprising combination of wooden planks and high-quality Bianco Statuario marble.

The interior work was carried out by Interieur Vandeputte (Proven, Poperinge).
Van den Weghe were responsible for the stonework.

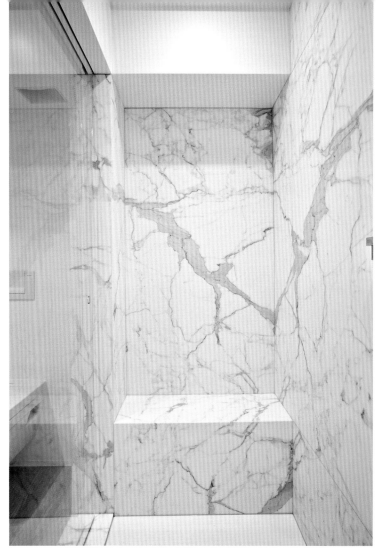

IXTRA Interior Architecture

Filip Vanryckeghem

 Ieperstraat 18

 B – 8930 Menen

 T/F +32 (0)56 530 457

 www.ixtra.be

 info@ixtra.be

VAN DEN WEGHE

The Stone Company

 Statiestraat 69

 B – 9870 Zulte

 T +32 (0)9 388 83 00

 F +32 (0)9 388 51 66

 www.vandenweghe.be

 info@vandenweghe.be

A TRENDSETTER
FOR EXCLUSIVE TILES

Over the past two decades, Devos has expanded to become a real trendsetter when it comes to high-quality tiles, with a range including handmade Moroccan zelliges, terra-cotta floor tiles, marble and glass mosaic and river stones.

The company's installation service, with professional and experienced staff, directed by the head of the company, ensures a first-class finish in every kitchen, bathroom or swimming pool. Devos guarantees short delivery times and absolute adherence to deadlines.
Excellent after-service care and professional tips for maintenance are additional plus points.

A visit to the Devos showroom is definitely worthwhile: in a space of around 1000m2 the visitor can find a great many inspiring examples and a centre where creative combinations of materials can be devised.

In this report, the Devos tile company presents four recent projects involving unusual and exclusive materials.

p. 172-175
Hand-cut Italian glass mosaic was selected for this bathroom.

A monochrome white bathroom finished by Devos in marble mosaic (Atrium Alize in Greek Thassos marble).

A shower in natural cubic basalt.

Shower and walls in river stones.

DEVOS TILES

Hoevestraat 35
B – 8500 Kortrijk
T +32 (0)56 24 90 10
F +32 (0)56 25 99 48
www.devostegelbedrijf.be
info@devostegelbedrijf.be

VARIATIONS ON A THEME

In this report, the stone company Van den Weghe presents four projects carried out in collaboration with three different designers.

They are variations based upon the same theme: the effective use of exclusive natural stone in bathrooms with unusual designs.

p. 182-185

For this bathroom, designer Magali Van den Weghe selected a bush-hammered Carrara marble and matt-grey granite.

The hammam has an arched ceiling. Infrared lamps have been installed in the shower.

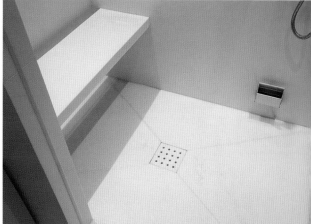

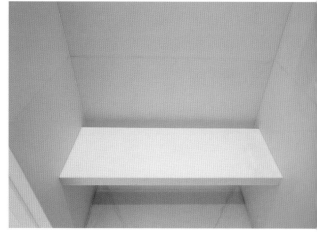

p. 186-189

These bathrooms were designed and created by Devaere nv.

The first project is in white Lasa marble throughout. For the second bathroom, Devaere selected Bisazza glass mosaic with a surface in composite Silestone.

Everything was installed by Van den Weghe.

p. 190-193

Dark natural stone (a Gris Sau bluestone) creates a cosy atmosphere in this project by Bert Desmet.

VAN DEN WEGHE
The Stone Company
   Statiestraat 69
   B – 9870 Zulte
   T +32 (0)9 388 83 00
   F +32 (0)9 388 51 66
   www.vandenweghe.be
   info@vandenweghe.be

SUBDUED AND SERENE

Stephanie Laporte studied interior architecture in Doornik and then started work at the famous Bataille & ibens studio in Antwerp.

At the end of 1999, she turned freelance, and two years later she combined forces with Jan Demeyere (architect) and Kris Carton (engineer/architect) to found The Office Belgium. The company has three departments: architecture, project management and interior architecture.
The following year, the trio also set up The Office Poland, and, together with business partner Hendrik Danneels, The Office Romania.

Stephanie Laporte's interiors are sleek and simple, but also radiate a sense of subdued elegance.
The bathrooms and bedrooms in this report are excellent examples of her sober, serene style and her passion for beautiful materials, light and texture.

THE OFFICE BELGIUM

    Veemarkt 37

    B – 8500 Kortrijk

    T +32 (0)56 326 108

    F +32 (0)56 326 109

    laporte.partners@telenet.be

THE OFFICE ROMENIA

    1 Ion Ionescu de la Brad Street, 6th floor

    Bucharest, sector 1

    Romenia

THE OFFICE POLAND SP. Z.O.O.

    Al. Jerozolemskie 212A

    02-486 Warszawa

    Poland

ADDRESSES

An Esther Gutmer project.

APLUZ (creative group)
Alexis Herbosch, Interior architect
Van Noortstraat 31
B – 2018 Antwerpen
T +32 (0)3 293 60 04
F +32 (0)3 293 60 05
www.apluz.be
contact @ apluz.be
p. 78-87

BRUCE BANANTO
145 W. 28th ST.
Suite 803
New York, NY 10001
T +1 212 563 1750
F +1 646 416 6218
p. 30-35

C&C DESIGNBURO
Martine Cammaert
Alfons Minoodtlaan 8
B – 9030 Mariakerke
T +32 (0)9 227 03 79
F +32 (0)9 227 78 29
c.c.designburo@skynet.be
p. 136-143

COSTERMANS
Dwarsdreef 52
B – 2970 Schilde
T +32 (0)3 385 02 44
F +32 (0)3 384 29 66
www.costermans-projecten.be
info@costermans-projecten.be
p. 62-77, p. 88-95

DEVOS Tiles
Hoevestraat 35
B – 8500 Kortrijk
T +32 (0)56 24 90 10
F +32 (0)56 25 99 48
www.devostegelbedrijf.be
info@devostegelbedrijf.be
p. 172-181

DTJ-Interior architect
Dennis T'Jampens
Opstal 37
B - 2650 Edegem
MOB +32 (0) 479 805 179
www.dtj-interiorarchitect.be
dennis@dtj-interiorarchitect.be
p. 150-153

EA2
European Architectural Antiques
26 Heistgoorstraat
B – 2220 Antwerpen / Heist op den Berg
T +1 617 894 04 95
info@ea2.be
p. 30-35

EBONY
Gilles de Meulemeester
132 av. Louise
B – 1050 Bruxelles
T +32 (0)2 646 86 02
F +32 (0)2 649 52 61
64 Boulevard Malesherbes
F – 75008 Paris
T +33 (0)1 42 93 75 06
www.ebony-interiors.com
ebony@ebony-interiors.com
p. 22-29

HUNTFORANTIQUES.COM
4 Itegembaan
B – 2580 Antwerpen / Putte
T +32 (0)477 56 03 38
p. 30-35

IL ETAIT UNE FOIS ...
Place du Châtelain, 10
B – 1050 Brussels
T +32 (0)2 537 07 05
F +32 (0)2 537 63 07
MOB +32 (0)475 787 133 (Anne De Visscher)
+32 (0)475 488 713 (Eric Meert)
+32 (0)476 50 44 21 (Catherine Mahieu)
www.iletaitunefois.be
iletaitunefois@skynet.be
Van Bunnenlaan 10
B – 8300 Knokke
p. 106-109

IXTRA INTERIEURARCHITECTUUR
Filip Vanryckeghem
Ieperstraat 18
B – 8930 Menen
MOB. +32 (0)474 311 974
T+F +32 (0)56 53 04 57
www.ixtra.be
info@ixtra.be
p. 154-171

LEROU
Monnikenwerve 131
Industriezone Blauwe Toren
B – 8000 Brugge
T +32 (0)50 31 74 42
F +32 (0)50 31 01 60
www.lerou.com
info@lerou.com
p. 128-133

DE MENAGERIE
Luc Lormans sprl
Leo de Bethunelaan 45
B – 9300 Aalst
T +32 (0)53 78 69 39
F +32 (0)53 70 79 96
MOB +32 (0)475 76 84 15
www.demenagerie.be
info@demenagerie.be
p. 96-99

CY PEYS
Interior Architects
Timmerwerfstraat 1
B – 2000 Antwerpen
T +32 (0)3 248 67 50
F +32 (0)3 248 39 55
www.cypeys.com
info@cypeys.com
p. 144-149

SIMONI INTERIOR ARCHITECTURE
Hentjenslaan 9-11
B – 3511 Hasselt
T +32 (0)11 25 35 02
F +32 (0)11 87 21 00
www.simoni.be
simoni@simoni.be
p. 40-61

SWYZEN
Interior Architecture
Elsdonklaan 26
B – 2610 Wilrijk
T +32 (0)3 281 13 22
F +32 (0)3 230 38 56
marianne@swyzen.be
p. 118-123

THEMENOS cvba
Sint-Jansvliet 8
B – 2000 Antwerpen
T +32 (0)3 248 49 93

F +32 (0)3 248 56 23
www.themenos.be
p. 16-21

THE OFFICE BELGIUM
Veemarkt 37
B – 8500 Kortrijk
T +32 (0)56 326 108
F +32 (0)56 326 109
laporte.partners@telenet.be
The Office Romenia
1 Ion Ionescu de la Brad Street, 6th floor
Bucharest, sector 1
Romenia
The Office Poland Sp. Z.O.O.
Al. Jerozolemskie 212A
02-486 Warszawa
Poland
p. 194-199

VAN DEN WEGHE
The Stone Company
Statiestraat 69
B – 9870 Zulte
T +32 (0)9 388 83 00
F +32 (0)9 388 51 66
www.vandenweghe.be
info@vandenweghe.be
p. 40-61, 100-105, 110-117,
154-171, 182-193

HANS VERSTUYFT ARCHITECTS
Van Bréestraat 35
B-2018 Antwerpen
T +32 (0)3 485 6762
F +32 (0)3 485 6764
www.hansverstuyftarchitecten.be
mail@hansverstuyftarchitecten.be
p. 36-39

WATERL'EAU
Schuttershofstraat 47
B – 2000 Antwerpen
T +32 (0)3 226 75 86
F +32 (0)3 226 75 93
info@waterleau-shop.be
Naamsestraat 9
B – 1000 Brussel
T/F +32 (0)2 513 24 00
waterleau-bxl@skynet.be
www.waterleau-shop.be
p. 118-127

PUBLISHER

BETA-PLUS Publishing

Termuninck 3

B - 7850 Enghien (Belgium)

T +32 (0)2 395 90 20

F +32 (0)2 395 90 21

www.betaplus.com

info@betaplus.com

PHOTOGRAPHY

All pictures: Jo Pauwels, except:

p. 62-77 : Patrick Verbeeck

GRAPHIC DESIGN

POLYDEM

Nathalie Binart

TRANSLATION

Laura Watkinson

February 2008

ISBN 13: 978 90 77213 88 9